CONTENTS

Learning Made Fun

Worm Cookies

- 1¾ cups all-purpose flour
- ¾ cup powdered sugar
- ¼ cup unsweetened cocoa powder
- ⅛ teaspoon salt
- 1 cup (2 sticks) butter, softened
- 1 teaspoon vanilla
- 1 tube white frosting

1. Combine flour, sugar, cocoa and salt; set aside. Combine butter and vanilla in large bowl. Beat with electric mixer at medium-low speed until fluffy. Gradually beat in flour mixture until well combined. Cover and chill dough at least 30 minutes before rolling.

2. Preheat oven to 350°F. Form dough into 1½-inch balls. Roll balls gently to form 5- to 6-inch logs about ½ inch thick. Shape into worms 2 inches apart on ungreased cookie sheets.

3. Bake 12 minutes or until set. Let stand on cookie sheets until cooled completely. Create eyes and stripes with white frosting.

Makes about 3 dozen cookies

Butterfly Cookies

2¼ cups all-purpose flour

¼ teaspoon salt

1 cup sugar

¾ cup (1½ sticks) butter, softened

1 egg

1 teaspoon vanilla

1 teaspoon almond extract

White frosting, assorted food colorings, colored sugars, assorted small decors, gummy fruit and hard candies for decoration

1. Combine flour and salt in medium bowl; set aside.

2. Beat sugar and butter in large bowl at medium speed of electric mixer until fluffy. Beat in egg, vanilla and almond extract. Gradually add flour mixture. Beat at low speed until well blended. Divide dough in half. Cover; refrigerate 30 minutes or until firm.

3. Preheat oven to 350°F. Grease cookie sheets. Roll half of dough on lightly floured surface to ¼-inch thickness. Cut dough with butterfly cookie cutters. Repeat with remaining dough. Transfer cutouts to ungreased cookie sheets.

4. Bake 12 to 15 minutes or until edges are lightly browned. Remove to wire racks; cool completely.

5. Tint portions of white frosting with assorted food colorings. Spread desired colors of frosting over cookies. Decorate as desired.

Makes about 20 to 22 cookies

Honey Bees

- ¾ cup shortening
- ½ cup sugar
- ¼ cup honey
- 1 egg
- ½ teaspoon vanilla
- 2 cups all-purpose flour
- ⅓ cup cornmeal
- 1 teaspoon baking powder
- ½ teaspoon salt
- Yellow and black decorating icings or gels, gummy fruit and decors

1. Beat shortening, sugar and honey in large bowl at medium speed of electric mixer until fluffy. Add egg and vanilla; mix until well blended. Combine flour, cornmeal, baking powder and salt in medium bowl. Add to shortening mixture; mix at low speed until well blended. Shape dough into disc. Wrap in plastic wrap; refrigerate 2 hours or overnight.

2. Preheat oven to 375°F. Divide dough into 24 equal sections. Shape each section into oval-shaped ball. Place 2 inches apart on ungreased cookie sheets.

3. Bake 10 to 12 minutes or until lightly browned. Cool 2 minutes on cookie sheets. Remove to wire racks; cool completely.

4. Decorate cookies with icings, gummy fruit and decors to resemble honey bees. *Makes 2 dozen cookies*

Domino Cookies

    1 package (20 ounces) refrigerated sugar cookie dough
      All-purpose flour (optional)
    ½ cup semisweet chocolate chips

1. Preheat oven to 350°F. Grease cookie sheets.

2. Remove dough from wrapper according to package directions. Cut dough into 4 equal sections. Reserve 1 section; refrigerate remaining 3 sections.

3. Roll reserved dough to ⅛-inch thickness. Sprinkle with flour to minimize sticking, if necessary. Cut out 9 (2½×1¾-inch) rectangles using sharp knife. Place 2 inches apart on prepared cookie sheets.

4. Score each cookie across middle with sharp knife. Gently press chocolate chips, point side down, into dough to resemble various dominos. Repeat with remaining dough, scraps and chocolate chips.

5. Bake 8 to 10 minutes or until edges are light golden brown. Remove to wire racks; cool completely.   *Makes 3 dozen cookies*

Tip: Use these adorable cookies as a learning tool for kids. They can count the number of chocolate chips in each cookie and arrange them in lots of ways: highest to lowest, numerically or even solve simple math problems. As a treat, they can eat the cookies afterwards.

Musical Instrument Cookies

1 package (18 ounces) refrigerated sugar cookie dough
All-purpose flour (optional)
Assorted colored frostings, colored gels, colored sugars, candy and small decors

1. Preheat oven to 350°F. Grease cookie sheets.

2. Remove dough from wrapper according to package directions. Divide dough into 2 equal sections. Reserve 1 section; cover and refrigerate remaining section.

3. Roll reserved dough on lightly floured surface to ¼-inch thickness. Sprinkle with flour to minimize sticking, if necessary. Cut out cookies using about 3½-inch musical notes and instrument cookie cutters. Place cookies 2 inches apart on prepared cookie sheets. Repeat with remaining dough.

4. Bake 10 to 12 minutes or until edges are lightly browned. Remove from oven. Cool on cookie sheets 2 minutes. Remove to wire racks; cool completely.

5. Decorate with colored frostings, gels, sugars and assorted decors as shown in photo. *Makes about 2 dozen cookies*

hint:
When making cutout cookies, dip the cookie cutters in flour before each use. That way the cookie dough will not stick to the cookie cutters.

Peanut Butter Bears

- 2 cups uncooked quick oats
- 2 cups all-purpose flour
- 1 tablespoon baking powder
- 1 cup granulated sugar
- ¾ cup (1½ sticks) butter, softened
- ½ cup creamy peanut butter
- ½ cup packed brown sugar
- ½ cup cholesterol-free egg substitute
- 1 teaspoon vanilla
- 3 tablespoons miniature chocolate chips

1. Combine oats, flour and baking powder in medium bowl; set aside.

2. Beat granulated sugar, butter, peanut butter and brown sugar in large bowl with electric mixer at medium-high speed until creamy. Add egg substitute and vanilla; beat until light and fluffy. Add oat mixture. Beat on low speed until combined. Cover and refrigerate 1 to 2 hours or until easy to handle.

3. Preheat oven to 375°F.

4. For each bear, shape one 1-inch ball for body and one ¾-inch ball for head. Place body and head together on cookie sheet; flatten slightly. Form 7 small balls for ears, arms, legs and mouth; arrange on bear body and head. Place 2 chocolate chips on each head for eyes; place 1 chocolate chip on each body for belly-button.

5. Bake 9 to 11 minutes or until edges are lightly browned. Cool 1 minute on cookie sheet. Remove to wire racks; cool completely.

Makes 4 dozen cookies

Peanut Butter Bear

Crayon Cookies

1 cup (2 sticks) butter, softened
2 teaspoons vanilla
½ cup powdered sugar
2¼ cups all-purpose flour
¼ teaspoon salt
    Assorted paste food colorings
1½ cups chocolate chips
1½ teaspoons shortening

1. Preheat oven to 350°F. Grease cookie sheets.

2. Beat butter and vanilla in large bowl at high speed of electric mixer until fluffy. Add powdered sugar; beat at medium speed until blended. Combine flour and salt in small bowl; add gradually to butter mixture until combine.

3. Divide dough into 10 equal sections. Reserve 1 section; cover and refrigerate remaining 9 sections. Combine reserved section and desired food coloring in small bowl; blend well.

4. Cut dough section in half. Roll each half into 5-inch log. Pinch one end to resemble crayon tip. Place cookies 2 inches apart on prepared cookie sheets. Repeat with remaining 9 sections of dough and desired food colorings.

5. Bake 15 to 18 minutes or until edges are lightly browned. Cool completely on cookie sheets.

6. Combine chocolate chips and shortening in small microwavable bowl. Microwave at HIGH 1 to 1½ minutes, stirring after 1 minute, or until chocolate is melted and smooth. Decorate cookies with chocolate mixture to look like crayons. *Makes 20 cookies*

Nutty Footballs

    1 cup (2 sticks) butter, softened
    ½ cup sugar
    1 egg
    ½ teaspoon vanilla
    2 cups all-purpose flour
    ¼ cup unsweetened cocoa powder
    1 cup finely chopped almonds
        Prepared colored decorating icings (optional)
        Prepared white decorating icing

1. Beat butter and sugar in large bowl at medium speed of electric mixer until creamy. Add egg and vanilla; mix until well blended. Combine flour and cocoa; gradually add to butter mixture, beating until well blended. Add almonds; beat until well blended. Shape dough into disc. Wrap in plastic wrap; refrigerate 30 minutes.

2. Preheat oven to 350°F. Lightly grease cookie sheets. Roll out dough on floured surface to ¼-inch thickness. Cut dough with 2½- to 3-inch football-shaped cookie cutter.* Place 2 inches apart on prepared cookie sheets.

3. Bake 10 to 12 minutes or until set. Cool on cookie sheets 1 to 2 minutes. Remove to wire rack; cool completely. Decorate with colored icings, if desired. Pipe white icing onto footballs to make laces.   *Makes 2 dozen cookies*

*To make football shapes without a cookie cutter, shape 3 tablespoonfuls of dough into ovals. Place 3 inches apart on prepared cookie sheets. Flatten ovals to ¼-inch thickness; taper ends. Bake as directed.

Baseball Caps

   1 cup butter (2 sticks), softened
   7 ounces almond paste
   ¾ cup sugar
   1 egg
   1 teaspoon vanilla
   ¼ teaspoon salt
   3 cups all-purpose flour
   Assorted colored decorating icings and colored candies

1. Preheat oven to 350°F. Grease cookie sheets. Beat butter, almond paste, sugar, egg, vanilla and salt in large bowl at high speed of electric mixer until light and fluffy. Add flour all at once; stir just to combine.

2. Roll ¼ of dough on lightly floured surface to ⅛-inch thickness. Cut out 1-inch circles. Place cutouts 2 inches apart on prepared cookie sheets.

3. Shape remaining dough into 1-inch balls.* Place one ball on top of dough circle so about ½ inch of circle sticks out to form bill of baseball cap. Repeat with remaining dough balls and circles.

4. Bake 10 to 12 minutes or until lightly browned. If bills brown too quickly, cut small strips of foil and cover with shiny side of foil facing up. Let cool on cookie sheets 2 minutes. Remove to wire racks; cool completely. Decorate with icings and candies as desired.

Makes about 3 dozen cookies

Use 1-tablespoon scoop to keep baseball caps uniform in size and professional looking.

Checkerboard Cookie

 1 cup sugar

 ¾ cup (1½ sticks) butter, softened

 2 eggs

 1 teaspoon vanilla

2¾ cups self-rising flour

 All-purpose flour

 Red and black decorating icings

1. Beat sugar and butter in large bowl at high speed of electric mixer until light and fluffy. Add eggs and vanilla; stir to combine. Add self-rising flour; stir until just combined. Cover and refrigerate 30 minutes.

2. Preheat oven to 350°F. Grease cookie sheets.

3. Roll ¼ of dough on lightly floured surface to ¼-inch thickness. Cut 24 circles with 1-inch round cookie cutter. Place on prepared cookie sheets.

4. Bake 8 to 10 minutes or until cookies turn light golden brown. Cool on cookie sheet 2 minutes. Remove to wire rack; cool completely.

5. Combine scraps of dough with remaining dough. Roll on lightly floured surface to 12-inch square. Place on greased 15½×12-inch cookie sheet.

6. Bake 10 to 12 minutes or until middle does not leave indentation when lightly touched with fingertips. Cool on cookie sheet 5 minutes. Slide checkerboard onto wire rack; cool completely.

7. Divide surface of checkerboard into 8 equal rows containing 8 equal columns. Alternate every other square with red and black icing to create checkerboard. Spread red icing on 12 checker playing pieces and black on remaining 12 checker playing pieces. Allow pieces to stand until icing is set. Place red pieces on black squares and black pieces on red squares. *Makes 1 checkerboard cookie*

Chocolate Spiders

¼ cup (½ stick) butter, softened
1 package (12 ounces) semisweet chocolate chips
1 cup butterscotch-flavored chips
¼ cup creamy peanut butter
4 cups crisp rice cereal
Chow mein noodles and assorted candies

1. Line baking sheet with waxed paper.

2. Combine butter, chocolate and butterscotch chips in large saucepan; stir over medium heat until chips are melted and mixture is well blended. Remove from heat. Add peanut butter; mix well. Add cereal; stir to evenly coat.

3. Drop mixture by tablespoonfuls, onto prepared baking sheet; insert chow mein noodles for legs and add candies for eyes.

Makes about 3 dozen

Doughnut Hole Spiders: Substitute chocolate-covered doughnut holes for shaped cereal mixture. Insert black string licorice, cut into 1½-inch lengths, into doughnut holes for legs. Use desired color decorating icing to dot onto doughnut holes for eyes.

hint:
To add extra crunch to these delicious cookies, sprinkle in some chopped peanuts when you are stirring in the cereal.

Chip-a-licious

Cookie Pizza

1 (18-ounce) package refrigerated sugar cookie dough

2 cups (12 ounces) semi-sweet chocolate chips

1 (14-ounce) can EAGLE BRAND® Sweetened Condensed Milk (NOT evaporated milk)

2 cups candy-coated milk chocolate pieces

2 cups miniature marshmallows

½ cup peanuts

1. Preheat oven to 375°F. Press cookie dough into 2 ungreased 12-inch pizza pans. Bake 10 minutes or until golden. Remove from oven.

2. In medium saucepan, melt chips with Eagle Brand. Spread over crusts. Sprinkle with chocolate pieces, marshmallows and peanuts.

3. Bake 4 minutes or until marshmallows are lightly toasted. Cool. Cut into wedges. *Makes 2 pizzas (24 servings)*

Prep Time: 15 minutes
Bake Time: 14 minutes

7 - 6 = 1   4 - 2 = 2   8 - 3 = 5

Peanut Butter Chocolate Chippers

    1 cup packed light brown sugar

    1 cup creamy or chunky peanut butter

    1 large egg

    ¾ cup milk chocolate chips

    Granulated sugar

1. Preheat oven to 350°F.

2. Combine brown sugar, peanut butter and egg in medium bowl; mix until well blended. Add chips; mix well.

3. Roll heaping tablespoonfuls of dough into 1½-inch balls. Place balls 2 inches apart on ungreased cookie sheets.

4. Dip table fork into granulated sugar; press criss-cross fashion onto each ball, flattening to ½-inch thickness.

5. Bake 12 minutes or until set. Let cookies stand on cookie sheets 2 minutes. Remove cookies with spatula to wire racks; cool completely.

Makes about 2 dozen cookies

Note: This simple recipe is unusual because it doesn't contain any flour—but it still makes great cookies!

hint:

These cookies make delicious sandwich cookies, too. Spread the bottoms of half the cookies with your favorite icing, and then top with the remaining cookies. Press the cookies together slightly until the icing is spread between the cookies.

7 - 6 = 1   4 - 2 = 2   8 - 3 = 5

Original Nestlé® Toll House® Chocolate Chip Cookies

2¼ cups all-purpose flour

1 teaspoon baking soda

1 teaspoon salt

1 cup (2 sticks) butter or margarine, softened

¾ cup granulated sugar

¾ cup packed brown sugar

1 teaspoon vanilla extract

2 large eggs

2 cups (12-ounce package) NESTLÉ® TOLL HOUSE® Semi-Sweet Chocolate Morsels

1 cup chopped nuts

PREHEAT oven to 375°F.

COMBINE flour, baking soda and salt in small bowl. Beat butter, granulated sugar, brown sugar and vanilla extract in large mixer bowl until creamy. Add eggs, one at a time, beating well after each addition. Gradually beat in flour mixture. Stir in morsels and nuts. Drop by rounded tablespoon onto ungreased baking sheets.

BAKE for 9 to 11 minutes or until golden brown. Cool on baking sheets for 2 minutes; remove to wire racks to cool completely.

Makes about 5 dozen cookies

Pan Cookie Variation: GREASE 15×10-inch jelly-roll pan. Prepare dough as above. Spread into prepared pan. Bake for 20 to 25 minutes or until golden brown. Cool in pan on wire rack. Makes 4 dozen bars.

Slice and Bake Cookie Variation: PREPARE dough as above. Divide dough in half; wrap in wax paper. Refrigerate for 1 hour or until firm. Shape each half into 15-inch log; wrap in wax paper. Refrigerate for 30 minutes. *(Dough may be stored in refrigerator for up to 1 week or in freezer for up to 8 weeks.)* Preheat oven to 375°F. Cut into ½-inch-thick slices; place on ungreased baking sheets. Bake for 8 to 10 minutes or until golden brown. Cool on baking sheets for 2 minutes; remove to wire racks to cool completely. Makes about 5 dozen cookies.

7 - 6 = 1   4 - 2 = 2   8 - 3 = 5

Chocolate Crackletops

- 2 cups all-purpose flour
- 2 teaspoons baking powder
- 2 cups granulated sugar
- ½ cup (1 stick) butter or margarine
- 4 squares (1 ounce each) unsweetened baking chocolate, chopped
- 4 large eggs, lightly beaten
- 2 teaspoons vanilla extract
- 1¾ cups "M&M's"® Chocolate Mini Baking Bits
- Additional granulated sugar

Combine flour and baking powder; set aside. In 2-quart saucepan over medium heat combine 2 cups sugar, butter and chocolate, stirring until butter and chocolate are melted; remove from heat. Gradually stir in eggs and vanilla. Stir in flour mixture until well blended. Chill mixture 1 hour. Stir in "M&M's"® Chocolate Mini Baking Bits; chill mixture an additional 1 hour.

Preheat oven to 350°F. Line cookie sheets with foil. With sugar-dusted hands, roll dough into 1-inch balls; roll balls in additional granulated sugar. Place about 2 inches apart onto prepared cookie sheets. Bake 10 to 12 minutes. Do not overbake. Cool completely on wire racks. Store in tightly covered container.   *Makes about 5 dozen cookies*

Hershey's "Perfectly Chocolate" Chocolate Chip Cookies

2¼ cups all-purpose flour
⅓ cup HERSHEY'S Cocoa
1 teaspoon baking soda
½ teaspoon salt
1 cup (2 sticks) butter or margarine, softened
¾ cup granulated sugar
¾ cup packed light brown sugar
1 teaspoon vanilla extract
2 eggs
2 cups (12-ounce package) HERSHEY'S Semi-Sweet Chocolate Chips
1 cup chopped nuts (optional)

1. Heat oven to 375°F.

2. Stir together flour, cocoa, baking soda and salt. Beat butter, granulated sugar, brown sugar and vanilla in large bowl on medium speed of mixer until creamy. Add eggs; beat well. Gradually add flour mixture, beating until well blended. Stir in chocolate chips and nuts, if desired. Drop by rounded teaspoons onto ungreased cookie sheets.

3. Bake 8 to 10 minutes or until set. Cool slightly; remove from cookie sheets to wire rack.   *Makes about 5 dozen cookies*

7 - 6 = 1 4 - 2 = 2 8 - 3 = 5

Dreamy Chocolate Chip Cookies

1¼ cups firmly packed brown sugar

¾ Butter Flavor CRISCO® Stick or ¾ cup Butter Flavor CRISCO® all-vegetable shortening

3 eggs, lightly beaten

2 teaspoons vanilla

1 (4-ounce) package German sweet chocolate, melted, cooled

3 cups all-purpose flour

1 teaspoon baking soda

½ teaspoon salt

1 (11½-ounce) package milk chocolate chips

1 (10-ounce) package premium semisweet chocolate chips

1 cup coarsely chopped macadamia nuts

1. Heat oven to 375°F. Place sheets of foil on countertop for cooling cookies.

2. Combine brown sugar, ¾ cup shortening, eggs and vanilla in large bowl. Beat at low speed of electric mixer until blended. Increase speed to high. Beat 2 minutes. Add melted chocolate. Mix until well blended.

3. Combine flour, baking soda and salt. Add gradually to shortening mixture at low speed.

4. Stir in chocolate chips and nuts with spoon. Drop by rounded tablespoonfuls 3 inches apart onto ungreased baking sheets.

5. Bake at 375°F for 9 to 11 minutes or until set. *Do not overbake.* Cool 2 minutes on baking sheets. Remove cookies to foil to cool completely.   *Makes about 3 dozen cookies*

7 - 6 = 1   4 - 2 = 2   8 - 3 = 5

Peanut Butter and Chocolate Spirals

1 package (20 ounces) refrigerated sugar cookie dough

1 package (20 ounces) refrigerated peanut butter
   cookie dough

¼ cup unsweetened cocoa powder

⅓ cup peanut butter-flavored chips, chopped

¼ cup all-purpose flour

⅓ cup miniature chocolate chips

1. Remove each dough from wrapper according to package directions.

2. Place sugar cookie dough and cocoa in large bowl; mix with fork to blend. Stir in peanut butter chips.

3. Place peanut butter cookie dough and flour in another large bowl; mix with fork to blend. Stir in chocolate chips. Divide each dough in half; cover and refrigerate 1 hour.

4. Roll each dough on floured surface to 12×6-inch rectangle. Layer each half of peanut butter dough onto each half of chocolate dough. Roll up doughs, starting at long end to form 2 (12-inch) rolls. Wrap in plastic wrap; refrigerate 1 hour.

5. Preheat oven to 375°F. Cut dough into ½-inch-thick slices. Place cookies 2 inches apart on ungreased cookie sheets.

6. Bake 10 to 12 minutes or until lightly browned. Remove to wire racks; cool completely.   *Makes 4 dozen cookies*

hint:

Use gentle pressure and a back-and-forth sawing motion when slicing rolls of refrigerator dough. The cookies will keep their nice round shape.

7 - 6 = 1   4 - 2 = 2   8 - 3 = 5

Hershey's Milk Chocolate Chip Giant Cookies

¼ cup plus 2 tablespoons butter, softened

½ cup granulated sugar

¼ cup packed light brown sugar

½ teaspoon vanilla extract

1 egg

1 cup all-purpose flour

½ teaspoon baking soda

2 cups (11½-ounce package) HERSHEY'S Milk Chocolate Chips

Frosting (optional)

Ice cream (optional)

1. Heat oven to 350°F. Line two 9-inch round baking pans with foil, extending foil over edges of pans.

2. Beat butter, granulated sugar, brown sugar and vanilla until fluffy. Add egg; beat well. Stir together flour and baking soda; gradually add to butter mixture, beating until well blended. Stir in milk chocolate chips. Spread one half of batter into each prepared pan, spreading to 1 inch from edge. (Cookies will spread to edge when baking.)

3. Bake 18 to 22 minutes or until lightly browned. Cool completely; carefully lift cookies from pans and remove foil. Frost, if desired. Cut each cookie into wedges; serve topped with scoop of ice cream, if desired. *Makes about 12 to 16 servings*

Tip: Bake cookies on the middle rack of the oven, one pan at a time. Uneven browning can occur if baking on more than one rack at the same time.

7 - 6 = 1 4 - 2 = 2 8 - 3 = 5

Colorific Chocolate Chip Cookies

- 1 cup (2 sticks) butter or margarine, softened
- ⅔ cup granulated sugar
- ½ cup firmly packed light brown sugar
- 1 large egg
- 1 teaspoon vanilla extract
- 2 cups all-purpose flour
- ¾ teaspoon baking soda
- ¾ teaspoon salt
- 1¾ cups "M&M's"® Semi-Sweet Chocolate Mini Baking Bits
- ¾ cup chopped nuts, optional

Preheat oven to 375°F. In large bowl cream butter and sugars until light and fluffy; beat in egg and vanilla. In medium bowl combine flour, baking soda and salt; blend into creamed mixture. Stir in "M&M's"® Semi-Sweet Chocolate Mini Baking Bits and nuts, if desired. Drop by heaping tablespoonfuls about 2 inches apart onto ungreased cookie sheets. Bake 9 to 12 minutes or until lightly browned. Cool 1 minute on cookie sheets; cool completely on wire racks. Store in tightly covered container.   *Makes about 3 dozen cookies*

Hint: For chewy cookies bake 9 to 10 minutes; for crispy cookies bake 11 to 12 minutes.

Pan Cookie Variation: Prepare dough as directed; spread into lightly greased 15×10×1-inch jelly-roll pan. Bake at 375°F for 18 to 22 minutes. Cool completely before cutting into 35 (2-inch) squares. For a more festive look, reserve ½ cup baking bits to sprinkle on top of dough before baking.

Chocolate Chip Cookie Bars

1¼ cups firmly packed light brown sugar

¾ Butter Flavor CRISCO® Stick or ¾ cup Butter Flavor CRISCO® all-vegetable shortening plus additional for greasing

2 tablespoons milk

1 tablespoon vanilla

2 eggs

1¾ cups all-purpose flour

1 teaspoon salt

¾ teaspoon baking soda

1 cup (6 ounces) semisweet chocolate chips

1 cup coarsely chopped pecans* (optional)

If pecans are omitted, add an additional ½ cup semisweet chocolate chips.

1. Heat oven to 350°F. Grease 13×9-inch baking pan. Place wire rack on countertop for cooling bars.

2. Combine brown sugar, ¾ cup shortening, milk and vanilla in large bowl. Beat at medium speed of electric mixer until well blended. Add eggs; beat well.

3. Combine flour, salt and baking soda. Add to shortening mixture; beat at low speed just until blended. Stir in chocolate chips and nuts, if desired.

4. Press dough evenly onto bottom of prepared pan.

5. Bake at 350°F for 20 to 25 minutes or until lightly browned and firm in the center. *Do not overbake.* Cool completely on cooling rack. Cut into 2×1½-inch bars.   *Makes about 3 dozen bars*

Bake Sale Treats

Ice Cream Cone Cupcakes

**1 package (18¼ ounces) white cake mix plus ingredients
to prepare**

2 tablespoons nonpareils*

**2 packages (1¾ ounces each) flat-bottomed ice cream cones
(about 24 cones)**

1 container (16 ounces) vanilla or chocolate frosting

Candies and other decorations

**Nonpareils are tiny, round, brightly colored sprinkles used for cake
and cookie decorating.*

1. Preheat oven to 350°F.

2. Prepare cake mix according to package directions. Stir in nonpareils.

3. Spoon ¼ cup batter into each ice cream cone.

4. Stand cones on cookie sheet. Bake cones until toothpick inserted
into center of cake comes out clean, about 20 minutes. Cool on wire
racks.

5. Frost each filled cone. Decorate as desired.

Makes 24 cupcakes

Note: Cupcakes are best served the day they are prepared. Store
loosely covered.

Ice Cream Cone Cupcakes

Indian Corn

- ¼ cup butter or margarine
- 1 package (10.5 ounces) mini marshmallows
- Yellow food coloring
- 8 cups peanut butter and chocolate puffed corn cereal
- 10 lollipop sticks
- 1 cup candy-coated chocolate pieces
- Tan and green raffia

1. Line large baking sheet with waxed paper; set aside. Melt butter in large heavy saucepan over low heat. Add marshmallows; stir until melted and smooth. Tint with food coloring until desired shade is reached. Add cereal and ½ cup chocolate pieces; stir until evenly coated. Remove from heat.

2. With lightly greased hands, quickly divide mixture into 10 oblong pieces. Push lollipop stick halfway into each oblong piece; shape like ear of corn. Place on prepared baking sheet; press remaining ½ cup chocolate pieces into each "ear." Let treats set.

3. Tie or tape raffia to lollipop sticks to resemble corn husks.

Makes 10 servings

hint:

Food colorings are edible dyes, usually red, green, blue and yellow. The most popular are liquid colors, which are available in supermarkets. They impart intense color and should initially be used sparingly, a drop or two at a time.

Old-Fashioned Cake Doughnuts

3¾ cups all-purpose flour

1 tablespoon baking powder

1 teaspoon ground cinnamon

¾ teaspoon salt

½ teaspoon ground nutmeg

3 eggs

¾ cup granulated sugar

1 cup applesauce

2 tablespoons butter, melted

1 quart vegetable oil

2 cups sifted powdered sugar

3 tablespoons milk

½ teaspoon vanilla

Colored sprinkles (optional)

Combine flour, baking powder, cinnamon, salt and nutmeg in medium bowl. Beat eggs in large bowl with electric mixer at high speed until frothy. Gradually beat in granulated sugar. Continue beating at high speed 4 minutes until thick and lemon colored, scraping down side of bowl once. Reduce speed to low; beat in applesauce and butter.

Beat in flour mixture until well blended. Divide dough into halves. Place each half on large piece of plastic wrap. Pat each half into 5-inch square; wrap in plastic wrap. Refrigerate 3 hours or until well chilled.

To prepare glaze, stir together powdered sugar, milk and vanilla in small bowl until smooth. Cover; set aside.

Roll out 1 dough half to ⅜-inch thickness. Cut dough with floured 3-inch doughnut cutter; repeat with remaining dough. Reserve doughnut holes. Reroll scraps; cut dough again. Pour oil into large Dutch oven. Place deep-fry thermometer in oil. Heat oil over medium heat until thermometer registers 375°F. Adjust heat as necessary to maintain temperature at 375°F.

continued on page 48

Old-Fashioned Cake Doughnuts, continued

Place 4 doughnuts and holes in hot oil. Cook 2 minutes or until golden brown, turning often. Remove with slotted spoon; drain on paper towels. Repeat with remaining doughnuts and holes. Spread glaze over warm doughnuts; decorate with sprinkles, if desired.

Makes 12 doughnuts and holes

Jack-O'-Lantern Chili Cups

2 cans (11.5 ounces each) refrigerated corn breadstick dough (8 breadsticks each) *or* 3 cans (4.5 ounces each) refrigerated buttermilk biscuits (6 biscuits each)

1 can (15 ounces) mild chili with beans

1 cup frozen corn

6 slices Cheddar cheese

Olive slices, bell pepper and carrot pieces for decoration

1. Preheat oven to 425°F. Lightly grease 16 to 18 regular-size (2½-inch) muffin pan cups. Lightly roll out corn bread dough to press together perforations. Cut out 18 circles with 3-inch round cookie cutter. Press 1 circle onto bottom and 1 inch up side of each muffin cup.

2. Combine chili and corn in medium bowl. Fill each muffin cup with 1 tablespoon chili. Cut out 16 to 18 circles from cheese with 2 inch round cookie cutter; place rounds over chili mixture in cups. Decorate cheese with olive, bell pepper and carrot pieces to resemble jack-o'-lanterns. Bake 10 to 12 minutes or until corn bread is completely baked and cheese is melted.   *Makes about 8 servings*

White Chocolate Chunk Muffins

2½ cups all-purpose flour

1 cup packed light brown sugar

⅓ cup unsweetened cocoa powder

2 teaspoons baking soda

½ teaspoon salt

1⅓ cups buttermilk

¼ cup plus 2 tablespoons butter, melted

2 eggs, beaten

1½ teaspoons vanilla

1½ cups chopped white chocolate

Preheat oven to 400°F. Grease 12 (3½-inch) large muffin cups; set aside.

Combine flour, sugar, cocoa, baking soda and salt in large bowl. Combine buttermilk, butter, eggs and vanilla in small bowl until blended. Stir into flour mixture just until moistened. Fold in white chocolate. Spoon into prepared muffin cups, filling half full.

Bake 25 to 30 minutes or until toothpicks inserted into centers come out clean. Cool in pan on wire rack 5 minutes. Remove from pan. Cool on wire rack 10 minutes. Serve warm or cool completely.

Makes 12 large muffins

Yuletide Twisters

> 1 (6-ounce) package premier white baking bars
> 1 tablespoon plus 1 teaspoon fat-free (skim) milk
> 1 tablespoon plus 1 teaspoon light corn syrup
> 8 ounces reduced-salt pretzel twists (about 80)
>   Cookie decorations, colored sugar or chocolate sprinkles

1. Line baking sheet with waxed paper; set aside.

2. Melt baking bars in small saucepan over low heat, stirring constantly. Stir in skim milk and corn syrup. Do not remove saucepan from heat.

3. Holding pretzel with fork, dip 1 side of each pretzel into melted mixture to coat. Place, coated side up, on prepared baking sheet; immediately sprinkle with desired decorations. Refrigerate until firm, 15 to 20 minutes.   *Makes 10 servings*

Chocolate Twisters: Substitute semisweet chocolate chips for premier white baking bars.

Caramel Dippity Do's: Heat 1 cup nonfat caramel sauce and ⅓ cup finely chopped pecans in small saucepan until warm. Pour into small serving bowl. Serve with pretzels for dipping. Makes 8 servings (about 2 tablespoons each).

Chocolate Dippity Do's: Heat 1 cup nonfat hot fudge sauce and ⅓ cup finely chopped pecans or walnuts in small saucepan until warm. Pour into small serving bowl. Serve with pretzels for dipping. Makes 8 servings.

Nn Oo Pp Qq Rr Ss Tt Uu Vv Ww Xx Yy Zz

Pretty Posies

1 package (20 ounces) refrigerated sugar cookie dough
Orange and blue or purple food colorings
1 tablespoon colored sprinkles

1. Remove dough from wrapper. Reserve ⅝ of dough. Combine remaining dough, orange food coloring and sprinkles in small bowl; beat at medium speed of electric mixer until well blended. Shape into 7½-inch log. Wrap in plastic wrap; refrigerate 30 minutes or until firm.

2. Combine reserved dough and blue food coloring in large bowl; beat at medium speed of electric mixer until well blended. Shape dough into disc. Wrap with plastic wrap and refrigerate 30 minutes or until firm.

3. Roll out blue dough on waxed paper to 7½×6-inch rectangle on sheet of waxed paper. Place orange log in center of rectangle. Fold blue edges up and around orange log; press seam together. Roll gently to form smooth log. Wrap waxed paper around dough and twist ends to secure. Freeze log 20 minutes.

4. Preheat oven to 350°F. Lightly grease cookie sheets. Remove waxed paper from dough log. Cut log into ¼-inch slices. Place 2 inches apart on prepared cookie sheets. Using 2½-inch flower-shaped cookie cutter, cut slices into flowers; remove and discard dough scraps.

5. Bake 15 to 17 minutes or until edges are lightly browned. Remove to wire rack; cool completely.   *Makes about 1½ dozen cookies*

Jack-O-Lantern Snacks

1 package (8 ounces) cream cheese, softened
   Red and yellow food coloring
8 large slices dark pumpernickel bread
1 small green bell pepper
   Sliced Genoa salami

1. Place cream cheese in small bowl. Add 8 drops red and 6 drops yellow food coloring to turn cream cheese orange. Mix well and adjust color as desired.

2. Toast bread and allow to cool. Using large pumpkin cookie cutter or metal 1-cup measure, cut round shape from each slice of toast leaving "stem" on top. Spread cream cheese over toast to edges. Cut "stems" from green pepper and place over stem on toast. Cut triangle "eyes" and mouth with several "teeth" from sliced salami. Arrange over each pumpkin toast.   *Makes 8 servings*

hint:

These treats are great to serve as "finger food" at Halloween celebrations too! Just provide a green, black or orange napkin under each toast and they will be even easier for the kids to handle.

Smushy Cookies

1 package (20 ounces) refrigerated cookie dough, any flavor
All-purpose flour (optional)

Fillings
Peanut butter, multi-colored miniature marshmallows, assorted colored sprinkles, chocolate-covered raisins and caramel candy squares

1. Preheat oven to 350°F. Grease cookie sheets.

2. Remove dough from wrapper according to package directions. Cut into 4 equal sections. Reserve 1 section; refrigerate remaining 3 sections.

3. Roll reserved dough to ¼-inch thickness. Sprinkle with flour to minimize sticking, if necessary. Cut out cookies using 2½-inch round cookie cutter. Transfer to prepared cookie sheets. Repeat with remaining dough, working with 1 section at a time.

4. Bake 8 to 11 minutes or until edges are light golden brown. Remove to wire racks; cool completely.

5. To make sandwich, spread about 1½ tablespoons peanut butter on underside of 1 cookie to within ¼ inch of edge. Sprinkle with miniature marshmallows, sprinkles and candy pieces. Top with second cookie, pressing gently. Repeat with remaining cookies and fillings.

6. Just before serving, place sandwiches on paper towels. Microwave at HIGH 15 to 25 seconds or until fillings become soft.

Makes about 8 to 10 sandwich cookies

Tip: Invite the neighbor kids over on a rainy day to make these fun Smushy Cookies. Be sure to have lots of filling choices available so each child can create their own unique cookies.

Chocolate Bunny Cookies

1 (21-ounce) package DUNCAN HINES® Family-Style Chewy Fudge Brownie Mix

1 egg

¼ cup water

¼ cup vegetable oil

1⅓ cups pecan halves (96)

1 container DUNCAN HINES® Creamy Home-Style Dark Chocolate Fudge Frosting

White chocolate chips

1. Preheat oven to 350°F. Grease baking sheets.

2. Combine brownie mix, egg, water and oil in large bowl. Stir with spoon until well blended, about 50 strokes. Drop by level tablespoonfuls 2 inches apart on greased baking sheets. Place two pecan halves, flat-side up, on each cookie for ears. Bake at 350°F for 10 to 12 minutes or until set. Cool 2 minutes on baking sheets. Remove to cooling racks. Cool completely.

3. Spread Dark Chocolate Fudge frosting on one cookie. Place white chocolate chips, upside down, on frosting for eyes and nose. Dot each eye with frosting using toothpick. Repeat for remaining cookies. Allow frosting to set before storing cookies between layers of waxed paper in airtight container. *Makes 4 dozen cookies*

Tip: For variety, frost cookies with Duncan Hines® Vanilla Frosting and use semisweet chocolate chips for the eyes and noses.

Snack Time

Dipped, Drizzled & Decorated Pretzels

1 bag chocolate or flavored chips (choose semisweet, bittersweet, milk chocolate, green mint, white chocolate, butterscotch, peanut butter or a combination)

1 bag pretzel rods

Assorted toppings: jimmies, sprinkles, chopped nuts, coconut, toasted coconut, cookie crumbs, colored sugars (optional)

Microwave Directions

1. Place chips in microwavable bowl. (Be sure bowl and utensils are completely dry.) Cover with plastic wrap and turn back one corner to vent. Microwave at HIGH for 1 minute; stir. Return to microwave and continue cooking in 30-second intervals until chips are completely melted. Check and stir frequently.

2. Dip one half of each pretzel rod into melted chocolate and decorate, if desired. Roll coated end of several pretzels in toppings. Drizzle others with contrasting color/flavor melted chips. (Drizzle melted chocolate out of spoon while rotating pretzel, to get even coverage.)

3. Place decorated pretzels on cooling rack; set over baking sheet lined with waxed-paper. Let coating harden completely. Do not refrigerate.   *Makes about 2 dozen pretzels*

 duck
 bird
 pig

 bunny  doggy  kitty cat

Super Spread Sandwich Stars

- **1 Red or Golden Delicious apple, peeled, cored and coarsely chopped**
- **1 cup roasted peanuts**
- **⅓ cup honey**
- **1 tablespoon lemon juice**
- **1 teaspoon ground cinnamon**
- **Sliced sandwich bread**

For Super Spread, place chopped apple, peanuts, honey, lemon juice and cinnamon in food processor or blender. Pulse food processor several times until ingredients start to blend, occasionally scraping down the sides with rubber spatula. Process 1 to 2 minutes until mixture is smooth and spreadable.

For Sandwich Stars, use butter knife to spread about 1 tablespoon Super Spread on 2 slices of bread. Stack them together, spread side up. Top with third slice bread. Place cookie cutter on top of sandwich; press down firmly and evenly. Leaving cookie cutter in place, remove excess trimmings with your fingers or a butter knife. Remove cookie cutter. *Makes 1¼ cups spread (enough for about 10 sandwiches)*

Favorite recipe from **Texas Peanut Producers Board**

 duck bird  pig

Quick S'Mores

1 whole graham cracker
1 large marshmallow
1 teaspoon hot fudge sauce

1. Break graham cracker in half crosswise. Place one half on small paper plate or microwavable plate; top with marshmallow.

2. Spread remaining ½ of cracker with fudge sauce.

3. Place cracker with marshmallow in microwave. Microwave at HIGH 12 to 14 seconds or until marshmallow puffs up. Immediately place remaining cracker, fudge side down, over marshmallow. Press crackers gently to even out marshmallow layer. Cool completely.

Makes 1 serving

hint:

S'mores can be made the night before and wrapped in plastic wrap or sealed in a small plastic food storage bag. Store at room temperature until ready to pack in your child's lunch box the next morning.

Take-Along Snack Mix

    1 tablespoon butter or margarine
    2 tablespoons honey
    1 cup toasted oat cereal, any flavor
    ½ cup coarsely broken pecans
    ½ cup thin pretzel sticks, broken in half
    ½ cup raisins
    1 cup "M&M's"® Chocolate Mini Baking Bits

In large heavy skillet over low heat, melt butter; add honey and stir until blended. Add cereal, nuts, pretzels and raisins, stirring until all pieces are evenly coated. Continue cooking over low heat about 10 minutes, stirring frequently. Remove from heat; immediately spread on waxed paper until cool. Add "M&M's"® Chocolate Mini Baking Bits. Store in tightly covered container.

Makes about 3½ cups

 duck bird  pig

Caramel Popcorn Balls

16 cups plain popped popcorn (do not use buttered popcorn)
1 package (14 ounces) caramels, unwrapped
¼ cup butter
Pinch of salt
1⅔ cups shredded coconut
1 package (12 ounces) semisweet chocolate chips
10 to 12 lollipop sticks
Halloween sprinkles and decorations (optional)

1. Place popcorn in large bowl.

2. Place caramels and butter in medium saucepan over low heat. Cook and stir until caramels and butter are melted and smooth, about 5 minutes. Stir in salt and coconut. Remove caramel mixture from heat; pour over popcorn. With large wooden spoon, mix until popcorn is evenly coated. Let cool slightly.

3. Place chocolate chips in microwavable bowl. Microwave at HIGH 1 minute; stir. Microwave at HIGH for additional 30-second intervals until chips are completely melted, stirring after each 30-second interval. Stir until smooth.

4. When popcorn mixture is cool enough to handle, grease hands with butter or nonstick cooking spray. Shape popcorn mixture into baseball-sized balls; place 1 lollipop stick in each ball. Dip each popcorn ball into melted chocolate and roll in Halloween decorations, if desired. Place on waxed paper until chocolate is set.

Makes 10 to 12 balls

Variation: Pour melted chocolate over caramel popcorn mixture; mix by hand until popcorn is coated with chocolate. Spread evenly on baking sheet lined with waxed paper until chocolate is set.

Soft Pretzels

- **1 package (16 ounces) hot roll mix plus ingredients to prepare mix**
- **1 egg white**
- **2 teaspoons water**
- **2 tablespoons *each* assorted coatings: coarse salt, sesame seeds, poppy seeds, dried oregano leaves**

1. Prepare hot roll mix according to package directions.

2. Preheat oven to 375°F. Spray baking sheets with nonstick cooking spray; set aside.

3. Divide dough equally into 16 pieces; roll each piece with hands to form rope, 7 to 10 inches long. Place on prepared cookie sheets; form into desired shape (hearts, wreaths, pretzels, snails, loops, etc.).

4. Beat egg white and water in small bowl until foamy. Brush onto dough shapes; sprinkle each shape with 1½ teaspoons of one coating.

5. Bake until golden brown, about 15 minutes. Serve warm or at room temperature. *Makes 16 servings*

Fruit Twists: Omit coatings. Prepare dough and roll into ropes as directed. Place ropes on lightly floured surface. Roll out, or pat, each rope into rectangle, ¼ inch thick; brush each rectangle with about 1 teaspoon spreadable fruit or preserves. Fold each rectangle lengthwise in half; twist into desired shape. Bake as directed.

Cheese Twists: Omit coatings. Prepare dough and roll into ropes as directed. Place ropes on lightly floured surface. Roll out, or pat, each rope into rectangle, ¼ inch thick. Sprinkle each rectangle with about 1 tablespoon shredded Cheddar or other flavor cheese. Fold each rectangle lengthwise in half; twist into desired shape. Bake as directed.

 duck bird pig

Cinnamon Apple Chips

2 cups unsweetened apple juice

1 cinnamon stick

2 Washington Red Delicious apples

1. In large skillet or saucepan, combine apple juice and cinnamon stick; bring to a low boil while preparing apples.

2. With paring knife, slice off ½ inch from tops and bottoms of apples and discard (or eat). Stand apples on either cut end; cut crosswise into ⅛-inch-thick slices, rotating apple as necessary to cut even slices.

3. Drop slices into boiling juice; cook 4 to 5 minutes or until slices appear translucent and lightly golden. Meanwhile, preheat oven to 250°F.

4. With slotted spatula, remove apple slices from juice and pat dry. Arrange slices on wire racks, being sure none overlap. Place racks on middle shelf in oven; bake 30 to 40 minutes until slices are lightly browned and almost dry to touch. Let chips cool on racks completely before storing in airtight container.   *Makes about 40 chips*

Tip: There is no need to core apples because boiling in juice for several minutes softens core and removes seeds.

Favorite recipe from **Washington Apple Commission**

 duck

 bird

 pig

 bunny  doggy  kitty cat

Perfect Pita Pizzas

   2 whole wheat or white pita bread rounds
   ½ cup spaghetti or pizza sauce
   ¾ cup (3 ounces) shredded part-skim mozzarella cheese
   1 small zucchini, sliced ¼ inch thick
   ½ small carrot, peeled and sliced
   2 cherry tomatoes, halved
   ¼ small green bell pepper, sliced

1. Preheat oven to 375°F. Line baking sheet with foil; set aside.

2. Using small scissors, carefully split each pita bread round around edge; separate to form 2 rounds.

3. Place rounds, rough sides up, on prepared baking sheet. Bake 5 minutes.

4. Spread 2 tablespoons spaghetti sauce onto each round; sprinkle with cheese. Decorate with vegetables to create faces. Bake 10 to 12 minutes or until cheese melts. *Makes 4 servings*

Pepperoni Pita Pizzas: Prepare pita rounds, partially bake, and top with spaghetti sauce and cheese as directed. Place 2 small pepperoni slices on each pizza for eyes. Decorate with cut-up fresh vegetables for rest of face. Continue to bake as directed.

 duck

 bird

 pig

S'Mores on a Stick

1 (14-ounce) can EAGLE BRAND® Sweetened Condensed Milk (NOT evaporated milk), divided

1½ cups milk chocolate mini chips, divided

1 cup miniature marshmallows

11 whole graham crackers, halved crosswise

Toppings: chopped peanuts, mini candy-coated chocolate pieces, sprinkles

1. Microwave half of Eagle Brand in microwave-safe bowl at HIGH (100% power) 1½ minutes. Stir in 1 cup chips until smooth; stir in marshmallows.

2. Spread chocolate mixture evenly by heaping tablespoonfuls onto 11 graham cracker halves. Top with remaining graham cracker halves; place on waxed paper.

3. Microwave remaining Eagle Brand at HIGH (100% power) 1½ minutes; stir in remaining ½ cup chips, stirring until smooth. Drizzle mixture over cookies and sprinkle with desired toppings.

4. Let stand for 2 hours; insert a wooden craft stick into center of each cookie.   *Makes 11 servings*

Prep Time: 10 minutes
Cook Time: 3 minutes

 duck bird  pig

 bunny  doggy  kitty cat

Caramel Corn Apple-O's

      7 cups popped butter-flavor microwave popcorn
2¼ cups apple cinnamon cereal rings
   ½ cup chopped dried apples or apricots
   ¼ cup chopped nuts (optional)
      1 package (14 ounces) caramels, unwrapped
      1 to 2 tablespoons water*
      2 tablespoons butter or margarine
         Long cinnamon sticks or wooden craft sticks (optional)

Start with 1 tablespoon water and add more if needed for consistency. Fresher caramels will require less water.

1. Combine popcorn, cereal, apples and nuts, if desired, in large bowl.

2. Microwave caramels, water and butter at HIGH 2½ to 3 minutes, stirring at 1 minute intervals until melted and smooth.

3. Pour caramel over popcorn mixture, tossing with buttered wooden spoon to coat. Let set until just slightly warm.

4. Dampen hands and shape mixture into 8 balls. Shape balls around sticks, if desired. Place on lightly buttered waxed paper until ready to serve.   *Makes 8 balls*

78 Snack Time

Caramel Corn Apple-O's

 duck bird  pig

Bar-o-metrics

Crispy Rice Squares

3 tablespoons Dried Plum Purée (recipe follows) or prepared dried plum butter

1 tablespoon butter or margarine

1 package (10 ounces) marshmallows

6 cups crisp rice cereal

Colored nonpareils

Coat 13×9-inch baking pan with vegetable cooking spray. Heat Dried Plum Purée and butter in Dutch oven or large saucepan over low heat, stirring until butter is melted. Add marshmallows; stir until completely melted. Remove from heat. Stir in cereal until well coated. Spray back of wooden spoon with vegetable cooking spray and pat mixture evenly into prepared pan. Sprinkle with nonpareils. Cool until set. Cut into squares. *Makes 24 squares*

Dried Plum Purée: Combine 1⅓ cups (8 ounces) pitted dried plums and ¼ cup plus 2 tablespoons hot water in container of food processor or blender. Pulse on and off until dried plums are finely chopped and smooth. Store leftovers in a covered container in the refrigerator for up to two months. Makes 1 cup.

Favorite recipe from **California Dried Plum Board**

"Everything but the Kitchen Sink" Bar Cookies

1 package (18 ounces) refrigerated chocolate chip cookie dough

1 jar (7 ounces) marshmallow creme

½ cup creamy peanut butter

1½ cups toasted corn cereal

½ cup miniature candy-coated chocolate pieces

1. Preheat oven to 350°F. Grease 13×9-inch baking pan. Remove dough from wrapper according to package directions.

2. Press dough into prepared baking pan. Bake 13 minutes.

3. Remove baking pan from oven. Drop teaspoonfuls of marshmallow creme and peanut butter over hot cookie base.

4. Bake 1 minute. Carefully spread marshmallow creme and peanut butter over cookie base.

5. Sprinkle cereal and chocolate pieces over melted marshmallow and peanut butter mixture.

6. Bake 7 minutes. Cool completely on wire rack. Cut into 2-inch bars.

Makes 3 dozen bars

> **hint:**
>
> Bar cookies look best when they are cut into uniform sizes. Measure the bars with a ruler and use a knife to score the surface. Then cut the bars along the score lines with a sharp knife.

Peanut Butter and Jelly Crispies

½ Butter Flavor CRISCO® Stick or ½ cup Butter Flavor
CRISCO® all-vegetable shortening plus additional
for greasing

½ cup JIF® Crunchy Peanut Butter

½ cup granulated sugar

½ cup firmly packed light brown sugar

1 egg

1¼ cups all-purpose flour

½ teaspoon baking powder

½ teaspoon baking soda

¼ teaspoon salt

2 cups crisp rice cereal

Honey roasted peanuts, finely chopped (optional)

SMUCKER'S® Jelly, any flavor

1. Heat oven to 375°F. Grease 13×9×2-inch pan with shortening.
Place wire rack on countertop for cooling bars.

2. Combine ½ cup shortening, peanut butter, granulated sugar and
brown sugar in large bowl. Beat at medium speed of electric mixer
until well blended. Beat in egg.

3. Combine flour, baking powder, baking soda and salt. Add gradually
to creamed mixture at low speed. Beat until well blended. Add cereal.
Mix just until blended. Press into greased pan. Sprinkle with nuts,
if desired.

4. Score dough into bars about 2¼×2 inches. Press thumb in center
of each. Fill indentation with ¼ to ½ teaspoon jelly.

5. Bake at 375°F for 12 to 15 minutes or until golden brown. *Do not
overbake.* Remove pan to wire rack. Cool 2 to 3 minutes. Cut into
bars. Cool completely.   *Makes about 2 dozen bars*

Irish Flag Cookies

1½ cups all-purpose flour

1 teaspoon baking powder

½ teaspoon salt

¾ cup granulated sugar

¾ cup light brown sugar

½ cup (1 stick) butter, softened

2 eggs

2 teaspoons vanilla

1 package (12 ounces) semisweet chocolate chips

Prepared white frosting

Green and orange food coloring

1. Preheat oven to 350°F. Grease 13×9-inch baking pan. Combine flour, baking powder and salt in small bowl; set aside.

2. Beat granulated sugar, brown sugar and butter in large bowl with electric mixer at medium speed until light and fluffy. Beat in eggs and vanilla. Add flour mixture. Beat at low speed until well blended. Stir in chocolate chips. Spread batter evenly into prepared pan. Bake 25 to 30 minutes or until golden brown. Remove pan to wire rack; cool completely. Cut into 3¼×1½-inch bars.

3. Divide frosting among 3 small bowls. Tint 1 with orange food coloring and 1 with green food coloring. Leave remaining frosting white. Frost individual cookies as shown in photo.

Makes 2 dozen cookies

hint:

Use different colored icings to make other national flags. Try red, white and green for Mexico, red, white and blue for France or red, yellow and black for Germany.

Yuletide Linzer Bars

1⅓ cups butter, softened

¾ cup sugar

1 egg

1 teaspoon grated lemon peel

2½ cups all-purpose flour

1½ cups whole almonds, ground

1 teaspoon ground cinnamon

¾ cup raspberry preserves

Powdered sugar

Preheat oven to 350°F. Grease 13×9-inch baking pan.

Beat butter and sugar in large bowl at medium speed of electric mixer until creamy. Beat in egg and lemon peel until blended. Mix in flour, almonds and cinnamon until well blended.

Press 2 cups dough onto bottom of prepared pan. Spread preserves over crust. Press remaining dough, a small amount at a time, evenly over preserves.

Bake 35 to 40 minutes until golden brown. Cool in pan on wire rack. Sprinkle with powdered sugar; cut into bars. *Makes 36 bars*

Candy Bar Bars

¾ cup (1½ sticks) butter or margarine, softened

¼ cup peanut butter

1 cup firmly packed light brown sugar

1 teaspoon baking soda

2 cups quick-cooking oats

1½ cups all-purpose flour

1 egg

1 (14-ounce) can EAGLE BRAND® Sweetened Condensed Milk (NOT evaporated milk)

4 cups chopped candy bars (such as chocolate-covered caramel-topped nougat bars with peanuts, chocolate-covered crisp wafers, chocolate-covered caramel-topped cookie bars, or chocolate-covered peanut butter cups)

1. Preheat oven to 350°F. In large mixing bowl, combine butter and peanut butter. Add brown sugar and baking soda; beat well. Stir in oats and flour. Reserve 1¾ cups crumb mixture.

2. Stir egg into remaining crumb mixture; press firmly on bottom of ungreased 15×10×1-inch baking pan. Bake 15 minutes.

3. Pour Eagle Brand evenly over baked crust. Stir together reserved crumb mixture and candy bar pieces; sprinkle evenly over top. Bake 25 minutes or until golden. Cool. Cut into bars. Store covered at room temperature.   *Makes 4 dozen bars*

Prep Time: 20 minutes
Bake Time: 40 minutes

Rocky Road Bars

- **2 cups (12-ounce package) NESTLÉ® TOLL HOUSE® Semi-Sweet Chocolate Morsels,** *divided*
- **1½ cups all-purpose flour**
- **1½ teaspoons baking powder**
- **1 cup granulated sugar**
- **¼ cup plus 2 tablespoons (¾ stick) butter or margarine, softened**
- **1½ teaspoons vanilla extract**
- **2 large eggs**
- **2 cups miniature marshmallows**
- **1½ cups coarsely chopped walnuts**

PREHEAT oven to 375°F. Grease 13×9-inch baking pan.

MICROWAVE *1 cup* morsels in medium, uncovered, microwave-safe bowl on HIGH (100%) power for 1 minute. STIR. Morsels may retain some of their original shape. If necessary, microwave at additional 10- to 15-second intervals, stirring just until morsels are melted. Cool to room temperature. Combine flour and baking powder in small bowl.

BEAT sugar, butter and vanilla in large mixer bowl until crumbly. Beat in eggs. Add melted chocolate; beat until smooth. Gradually beat in flour mixture. Spread batter into prepared baking pan.

BAKE for 16 to 20 minutes or until wooden pick inserted in center comes out slightly sticky.

REMOVE from oven; sprinkle immediately with marshmallows, nuts and *remaining* morsels. Return to oven for 2 minutes or just until marshmallows begin to melt. Cool in pan on wire rack for 20 to 30 minutes. Cut into bars with wet knife. Serve warm.

Makes 2½ dozen bars

Acknowledgments

The publisher would like to thank the companies and organizations listed below for the use of their recipes and photographs in this publication.

California Dried Plum Board

Duncan Hines® and Moist Deluxe® are registered trademarks of Aurora Foods Inc.

Eagle Brand®

Hershey Foods Corporation

© Mars, Incorporated 2004

Nestlé USA

The J.M. Smucker Company

Texas Peanut Producers Board

Washington Apple Commission

Index